BENDERDRIVEL

as seen on the radio

Rocky van de Benderskum
String DingaLing
Olly Gark
Genevieve De BlancdeBlanc

Published by; A small piece of vegan cheese named Nutty

ISBN: 9798378454273
Imprint: Independently published

Cover design by: A benderskum
Library of String Number: 420 4 LyF3
Printed in a secret location not very far from where you were standing
when you first read this.
Don't Pass Audit Prg Uber Liebe René's Caine Master Master

Adapted from the radio by placing it on a block of
wood and banging a few nails into it.

I dedicate this book to you the reader
Have a great life

CONTENTS

THREEWORD

It really wasn't worth a four or maybe even a fore
But thought it best to mention so you would know the score
There are sweary words I just couldn't stop
Because of a thing called coffeeright
Which is like copyright but pure delight
It's tastier and this is in my genes
I prefer stuff made with better beans.

INTRO

I'd just like to finish before I've begun.

For once I get going you might want to run.

Or possibly shoot me with a gatling gun.

Although if you do I've already won.

I'm Rocky van de Benderskum.

I'm not Rocky from a movie or Chicken Run.

Long in the tooth and proper spun.

Yes, I write drivel but mostly for fun.

Sometimes because something has to be done.

Though my body is broken so I'm not the one.

Action now is needed so the bad gets undone.

Nonsense is often prophetic but probably not this one.

This one lost any meaning or point long before it begun.

Organic unsynthesized cinnamon bun.

That sounds like a heavenly overrun.

So, I'd just like to finish before I've begun.

DISTRACTION 101

Have aliens arrived for their own fatal attraction?

Or is it that just about everything is a distraction?

For instance, the balloon shot down by the states,

could have caused repercussions make no mistake.

They say it came from China, but the Chinese have denied.

The US said it wasn't the first balloon that
flew over them and spied.

China responded you spied on us so this is our tit for tat.

To down it cost a quarter of a million, what do you say to that?

Just like the 99 Luftballons from that song it actually wasn't red.

They were air balloons on the original unless
it's the UK version instead.

Never mind what colour they were its just suffice to say.

There more balloons shot down as well,
and they were silver-grey.

Now have you paid attention the future of the planet is at stake.

And if it continues on like this they may make a grave mistake.

I'm not just talking of Russia or the war they have with Ukraine.

The behaviours of some other world
leaders are positively insane.

Democratic People's Republic of Korea now that's an oxymoron.

United? States of America. Another if I ever saw one.

Two world leaders strutting around to
show whose balls are bigger.

The metaphorical red button looms like a finger on the trigger.

One fires one of its missiles into the sea near Japan.

Then said it was unexpected and earlier than planned.

The other one is preparing a ginormous military exercise.

With the world in peril from climate change that isn't very wise.

Blowing up bombs in the ocean can only have one result.

Destroying what lives in the water though
it really wasn't their fault.

One of them has a sister that ordered another three,

missiles are what I'm talking about straight into the sea.

So, if you look at the bigger picture, worldwide are many wars.

Here comes that virus with shoes sending out its spores.

Have you ever seen land where the armed forces have trained?

There isn't much life there its energy completely drained.

Multiply that exponentially and then the land is dead.

Here comes that virus with shoes, oh apologies I already said.

I think someone decided there's too many
people so let's have a war.

Some are thinking this is the end but what are they fighting for?

The answer is very simple not just blowing in the wind.

The question however fluctuates whatever it is they rescind.

I could just say as we all know the answer is 42.

But the question for that is 6 x 9 so even that's not true.

ACRONYMS

An acronym can take more time than the full words ever do.

Although being abbreviations they make the time lesser too.

Acronyms like ACAB and LOL and WTF for what the fuck.

Have clearly taken over and clearly run amuck.

My friend said he couldn't advertise my festive drivel show.

Because of a social media ban I just replied I know.

I said it was yesterday so don't you worry mate.

He said he'd wanted to hear it sad he was too late.

I told him it was repeated 9.30 on Monday again.

I then wrote PM then afterwards thought
I needed to further explain.

When I said PM I felt obliged to make it clear.

I never meant Prime Minister don't be surprised to hear.

Private Message or Project Manager I also didn't mean.

Nor Post Mistress, pre-Menstrual or even Protocol Machine.

He understood without all that my efforts were totally wasted.

I could have saved myself the bother but
luckily I'd cut and pasted.

So, you see it can take ages to make a point.

I should have given it a miss and simply rolled a joint.

Though having said that what I meant
when I simply said I should.

Was about how it used to be before my
life was changed for good.

Anyway, back to the acronyms so avoiding the melancholy.

My favourite one is LOL and stands for Lick Orange Lolly.

A COMPARISON

Jimlings or Zangloids?

Can you tell the difference?

Recently it came to my attention that people don't seem to know the difference between Jimlings and Zangloids so I'm hoping to clear that up with the following;

Jimlings are tiny little two legged creatures they look sort of humanoid, when I say tiny, I mean like the size of a large bumblebee.

They are greenish grey with shocking pink hair, long sharp teeth for eating brickdust porridge with, their staple food source.

They are a silicon based life form and the reason buildings crumble, especially in the older parts of town.

They move really fast too and just like spiders can weave their way through multiple dimensions at the same time, so unless they are stunned by cats they are proper hard to see and even then it's fleeting as they zip into a different dimension to escape.

They don't really wear clothes because they are so quick and it's the norm in their place in the multiverse.

They are somewhat of an enigma in so much as they come from everywhere whilst simultaneously not coming from anywhere.

Zangloids though come from a far distant planet called Zonglit they arrived here on Earth aeons ago all prepared for conquest. However their boffins had made miscalculations in a few very important areas;

Size they are tiny compared to us slightly smaller than Jimlings, about the size of a hornet mimic hoverfly like Volucella zonaria although they were much smaller when they first arrived.

Atmospheric density as I said they were tiny when they arrived due to the relative size of their planet and the much heavier gravity there. When they stepped out of their ships they immediately started expanding in size they had already ascertained the air was breathable and they wouldn't need space suits, they hadn't expected to become too big to get back in their ships to fly off in less than three hours. Luckily the rapid growing only went on for six hours otherwise goodness knows how big they'd be by now.

Although very advanced technologically with their semi organic space craft their weapons had not undergone such an advance, hence spears.

They wear gowns like priests that are just one huge (relative to their size) multi coloured iridescent paisley patterned sheet. Although when they first gain their sheet on their naming day it is plain green in colour, the colours are from their ability to spray iridescent paisley patterns from their fingertips.

It's common knowledge in cryptozoological circles that the person that invented paisley must have studied Zangloids, although the name of that person is lost in time and space like pissing in the shower.

It is easier to see them than Jimlings as they aren't as quick as due partly to the fact they can't do the inter-dimensional jiggory pokery. If they could there's not much chance you'd have ever seen them, the chances of which are slim anyway.

You will I've no doubt have seen their abandoned space craft in woodlands across the planet, although if you didn't know you wouldn't recognise them, they are what people believe are dried out tree roots laying on the surface.

Obviously, you can glean from the above that they are not a threat to our world thank goodness. We are enough of a threat ourselves we really don't need help with destroying where we live.

ANARCHY IN THE UK

I say that I'm an Anarchist and this I can conceive.

The end is nigh for this autocracy this I truly believe.

One dictionary definition of an anarchist didn't define it to me.

It said a person who believes in or tries to bring about anarchy.

That isn't a definition it's simply just loads of words.

The moon is made of cheese is not any less absurd.

I say that I'm an Anarchist and this is what I mean.

Don't want central government, dictator, king or queen.

My LANGUAGE might be savoury but I'm not a fucking twat.

It doesn't mean I want to smash, or burn down this or that.

I'll always believe in freedom, and always will refrain.

From smashing and burning everything
cos that would be insane.

I believe that we could organise to efficiently meet our needs.

Without historic hierarchies born of war and greed.

Anarchism wouldn't be the death of fair society.

That's occurring every day with government impropriety.

They think that we're all stupid, but this all has to stop.

Just look at all the people installed in what is called the top.

Anarchy isn't chaos but a gateway to real autonomy.

That's a nicer working model for building our economy.

With willing individual and active co-operation.

We'd be on a better road to a truly human nation.

Criminals, bankers, politicians and thieves.

Wouldn't be able to do what they please.

We'd govern locally with fully moral laws.

Not a distant gang of strangers with the usual age-old flaws.

Everyone could have their say everyone have a voice.

No policing by coercion but governance through choice.

I understand confusion because it's what we've learned.

Controlling propaganda from mainstream
media constantly churned.

Another way to keep us down and to them it's just a game.

As a cannabis activist I've seen it loads
and to me it's all the same.

BAD HAIR DAY

I so feel you with bad hair days I mean.

Having a face for radio my hair is rarely seen.

Obviously, those that have may still have
no idea what I'm saying.

It never stays in place no matter how much
it gets; you know...hair spraying.

It's like a hopeless snowflake falling into a fire.

Or a drunken bird singing on a telephone wire.

So basically, I ignore it which it often does to me.

Currently it's on a tropical beach looking at the sea.

I know right? It's been there for weeks it's alright for some.

It spends my money on beaches I have to live like a bum.

But not to worry it's bound to be short lived;
I mean enough is enough.

I have a plan that's a little bit drastic and maybe a little rough.

Hair today gone tomorrow I'm sure that's what they say.

My revenge is swift I'm going to be bald immediately today.

If it's cold now that I'm totally hairless I'll buy a purple hat.

With the money I make from selling my
hair and that is the end of that.

CHIMERA

My medical records state I'm a chimera if
you don't what one of them is.

Simply put I have dual DNA and I'm really not taking the piss.

Although I am male for all intents and purpose.

I'm also female hidden underneath the surface.

No, I'm not transgender or anything like that.

I'm just a simple benderskum with a faded purple hat.

I had a lot of chemo to keep the aunties at bay.

Then finally a lethal dose ready for the day.

A bone marrow transplant through a Hickman line.

Just like getting a bag of blood and I'd had them plenty of times.

So, the stem cells went straight to my heart.

Seeking anything damaged and that was the start.

Some repaired my cochlear at least it seems it to me.

When I go out amongst other people its way too noisily.

Now though I can hear music without any hearing aids.

And that above everything else is ace of fucking spades.

The rest I guess went to my bone marrow.

Its intended destination the margins are narrow.

The stem cells were harvested the previous day.

Then flown by aeroplane from the US of A.

It should have copied my own DNA.

But for some technical reason that wasn't the way.

So, on entering my bone marrow it took the DNA of the donor.

Probably part of the reason I became a remoaner.

Apologies I couldn't help it and it and as
you heard it obviously fits.

Unlike the thoughts of hashtag bregret by
those that wanted brexshit.

Anyway, back to chimera before I lose the thread.

I have now got female bone marrow I'd
sooner have this than be dead.

With female DNA in my blood but elsewhere male DNA too.

And genetically modified hormones I'm like a gender stew.

Every day my body is attacked by my female immune system.

I'd like to explain it more scientifically but
simply don't have that wisdom.

Suffice to say I'm chimera but not really a mythical beast.

In the scheme of things, no more cultured
than a plate of infected yeast.

Although because it's not really normal it
needs to be watched constantly.

Which begs the question why is it four years
since I've actually seen a GP.

The NHS is in dire straits which makes me think Jesus wept.

Nurses rely on foodbanks to eat because the

government are totally inept.

Fireman and teachers and doctors and many others too.

Are striking but not just for themselves but also for me and you.

Heating and food bills are through the roof.

Which all seems planned out if I'm telling the truth.

The costs of electricity and gas are so high, but
the government are lending a hand.

They caused the prices to be that high I'm
sure you must understand.

They take away more than what they return
with a clever sleight of hand.

It's like they are holding up our rights and
hitting them with a stick.

Well, that's the way it seems to me but maybe I'm just thick.

Soon we'll see the king get crowned with
pomp and circumstance.

Wasting taxpayers' money for what is
hopefully their very last dance.

People say they're a tourist attraction but personally I disagree.

Tourists get to look at the buildings as the royals you rarely see.

So sing a song a sixpence a pocket full of bugs.

They want to keep us divided and think that we are mugs.

FOOD FOR THE FUTURE

Food for the future is something we need to think about.

Plant your seeds and feed the soil before it's all worn out.

I rarely go to protests, and I never did holler and shout.

These days front line protesting is not the thing for me.

I'd rather earth my potatoes up and plant a lemon tree.

Then sit amongst the strawberries that I'll grow.

So, this is something that I think you all should know.

I'd grow strawberries even though I think they're vile.

But others love them, and I love to see people smile.

Vegetables and fruit grown in the soil not
missing that vital ingredient.

The absence of which in hydroponic farms
is maybe truly expedient.

Without this element in our diet, we can't
take all its vital nutrition.

So effectively making us weaker with no
need for a war of attrition.

The ingredient of course molybdenum I simply couldn't resist.

To remove it from our diet is a travesty and
I'm not just taking the piss.

If you thought the GMO was bad well that was way too crude.

It goes quite deep it's well thought out this wanton war on food.

With a lot of care, some understanding
and a fair bit of honest toil.

Instead of an empty landscape we could
end up with really good soil.

With hope for the future, we intend to grow exponentially.

Whilst beginning to treat our world more reverentially.

Without using chemicals that pollute and poison the ground.

Organic practices that are earth friendly, vegan and sound.

Trees bursting with fruit, bushes and hedges too.

Food for everyone enough for the whole year through.

ELECTRICKERY

I read this week in Belgium a new energy storage facility opens.

Here though the story is very different a system clearly broken.

In this country it seems renewable producers
get paid to switch them off.

Which has cost consumers one billion pounds
not a figure at which to scoff.

So why aren't they building these storage facilities here?

It's not that simple you can't put in bottles like beer.

According to what the experts say electricity cannot be stored.

But in Belgium it seems it can this surely can't be ignored.

I understand it cost investors thirty million to construct.

Companies not governments so paying
to switch off proper sucks.

It can store one hundred megawatts per hour.

Imagine what you could do with all that renewable power.

We could have many of these spread around
for all our energy needs.

But that would never go down well with
oil and gas companies' greed.

I mean we could get all our power from

solar and wind and wave.

Politicians kowtow to fossil fuel lobbyists
none of them are brave.

There were 636 of these corporate beasts
in Egypt at copout 27 recently.

An event that would never have been needed
if we treated our planet decently.

But hey ho we are humans and treat our world like shit.

Like a virus in shoes continuing to destroy
by ever increasing bits.

But back to this electricity that our experts say can't be stored.

Except it seems in Belgium so their
knowledge is blatantly flawed.

Tesla have been building these facilities worldwide.

Because that is a fact the experts must have lied.

We need to look at this differently confine fossil fuels to history.

It costs 3.8 billion pounds to build a gigafactory.

One hundred of these could power the
world was a recent calculation.

Instead of 37 for a broken app that could have
been a tenth of world power salvation.

Governments wasting our money like that they
are obviously not fit for purpose.

But they like their lopsided economy it's only there to usurp us.

The time is ripe for change though and change is needed soon.

Not some farcical target that's like howling at the moon.

Whenever they have a copout, previous targets they try to alter.

They always make such promises up
knowing they will only falter.

The one billion pounds I mentioned was only the past five years.

Paid for via our energy bills you shouln't be surprised to hear.

Yet the gas and oil producers make billions
in a couple of months.

You and I the consumer must be thought of by them as chumps.

The cost-of-living crisis is being blamed
now on workers on strike.

If things were the same as history there'd
be lots of their heads on spikes.

But workers aren't actually the ones to blame.

Its governments worldwide every single one the same.

They seem to want to rule with only a personal agenda.

Times like this I really miss when I still lived in me bender.

CHRISTMAS AND STUFF

Did you feel bloated on Christmas day?

I hope not much food was be thrown away.

Though I know it was it's always like that.

The one percents wallets continue to get fat.

While down at the bottom and out on the street.

There are too many people with only handouts to eat.

This one is not just blah, blah, blah, but a proper cast iron truth.

It's hard to keep it real when you live by nail and tooth.

I know cos I have been there and seen it through these eyes.

There's more to life than 9 to 5 that's slavery in disguise.

Millions are relying on foodbanks to supplement their diets.

Working people can't afford to eat but mostly keeping quiet.

Get all you need for 30p a day? I suggest you fucking try it.

Keep the nation malnourished and stay too weak to riot.

So now working folks are going on strike
for there is no other way.

The government said they'll negotiate on everything but pay.

When earnings don't rise with inflation
that's the same as a cut in wages.

Austerity driven virtual cuts for years now in very large stages.

We live in a classless society or that's what I grew up believing.

So to all my past mentors I ask this; which
one of us were you deceiving?

There is an obvious difference between the various classes.

If you haven't noticed that you clearly must need glasses.

As for all the so-called illegal migrants
formally known as refugees.

Stuck in unfit accommodation a breeding ground for disease.

Or even those still in Calais where I expect a few will freeze.

It seems the government want them all to get back in the sea.

Anyway, I hear people crying thinking about
our own poor and homeless folk.

Those ones you walk quickly passed on the
street your morality is a bit of a joke.

I'm pretty sure there have been homeless
here for many, many years.

More will be joining them very soon so wipe away your tears.

Now to the ghosts of Christmas present
from the corpses on your plate.

Bring peace and goodwill to everyone before it is too late.

But with Christmas dinner abundance and

the oh so festive food coma.

Eating on such an epic scale should earn you an avarice diploma.

I guess the landfill wildlife will soon have plenty to eat.

A time they've waited for all year long the annual festive treat.

Unlike some of their captive cousins
slaughtered for the Christmas table.

Because of the possible birth of a child apparently in a stable.

Ten million turkeys murdered and a quarter of a million geese.

To celebrate the arrival of the so called prince of peace.

DEATH PENALTY

Bring back the death penalty a clueless monster said.

Bring back plague and famine oh and then bring out your dead.

Recognising what they are up to is much
more than just being aware.

Calling it woke is an unfunny joke and
comes from a place of don't care.

Before they go it seems they're trying to bleed the country dry.

With nothing anyone can do about it except
watch the prices go sky high.

While oil companies are boasting of bigger and bigger profits.

The government don't tax them properly so
there is no way they'll stop it.

I know the following is impossible but listen to what I say.

If from January the first zero one you earned thirty grand a day.

Using simple mathematics you'll see the
following statement is true.

You'd have earned nearly a third of BP profits for 2022.

I wish they'd stop pretending they had our best interest at heart.

Just a box of tricks named politics I called it from the start.

Sing a song of sixpence a pocket full of bribes.

Ask a member of parliament a straightforward
question the answer often circumscribes.

DUMP SHIT IN THE SEA

We poison the rivers and dump shit in the sea.

Well at least the bit not filled with our plastic debris.

When I say we I mean us the human race.

We're all partly responsible not some unknown face.

How we've cared for our planet is a tragic disgrace.

Now they are talking of allowing fracking again.

If you ask me, to even consider that is insane.

When they started to do it up at Preston New Road.

The fracking machine was not on full load.

Earthquakes were measured at more than allowed.

Two is a company but three is a crowd.

They had to stop fracking because that was the law.

So, the government decided to allow it no more.

But now they're looking at starting it again.

Did I mention before that I think that's insane?

They say it will help with our energy needs.

Not to mention their corporate mate's greed.

The industry is dangerous and that's saying the least.

It leaves dead land that's no good for man nor beast.

Nothing will grow the land is rotten and dead.

I don't know about you but that's something I dread.

From fracking the greenhouse gas Methane is released.

Also ground level ozone breathing that you'll soon be deceased.

From strokes, heart attacks and asthma among others.

Premature babies and birth defects for any pregnant mothers.

Contaminating the fresh water supply
and making it radioactive.

Do people really vote for governments that
want this as common practice?

They say they need to drill for more oil in the North Sea.

Probably want to even open a coal mine or two or three.

They'll sell the land from under your no
remorse and no apology.

This is extremely unnecessary merely political ideology.

We have renewable alternatives water, wind and sun.

They produce clean power for all so why have we not begun.

There are a fair few wind farms and fields full of panels too.

With sufficient storage space they could
save energy for me and you.

People say that the alternatives do much more harm than good.

Not looking at fossil fuel damage even
though they really should.

Nuclear power is the future I also hear them say.

With a disregard to the cost the planet will have to pay.

Then take another look at renewables and this is hard to believe.

In the past decade wind farm operators have
more than a billion received.

To switch off or halve their output when the national grid is full.

To lobby for stuff as costly as that you've gotta have some pull.

Obviously, those lobbyists are from the oil industry.

They profit from the loss of others, or it seems that way to me.

They can afford whatever they want
having made so much profit.

They're right up there at the top of the
heap time to push them off it.

The governments of course support them
probably for backhand pay.

Or some other less obvious sweetener as
long as they get their way.

FRACKS BACK

The latest government ideas are just old
ones they've brought back.

Now they want to allow all the filthy frackers to frack.

Care for the environment is something they clearly lack.

If they haven't done it already the subsurface they will crack.

No doubt there will be earthquakes above
the current restriction.

So they'll just change the law again
parliamentary science fiction.

If the land starts to die there's plenty more of that.

They'll also make new rules drawn out of a hat.

They have no true direction this government without a clue.

Have plans for the environment but it's not a pleasant view.

They say they'll go ahead if they get local consent.

Bribing the local people for them is money well spent.

The companies will be offering one
thousand pounds recompense.

If that is what is called local consent the
world no longer makes sense.

So local consent really means a bribe.

In order to keep a damaging industry alive.

They say it's because Putin invaded Ukraine.

The same old tired rhetoric do they think we're all insane?

The fracking company quadzilla don't pay any UK tax.

This isn't wild conspiracy it's bona fide cast iron fact.

Fracking pollutes the land, the water and the air.

They know these things already but just don't seem to care.

They're giving out more licences probably
for monsters to drill for oil.

Not giving even the slightest thought to
when the country spoils.

We obviously knew that already though
from the water companies' S.O.P.

Not dealing with any of the sewage just dumping it in the sea.

They've done that shit for years but nowadays have permission.

This government is worse than cancer
without any hope of remission.

They are now standing in the way of the fabled net zero.

Whilst the bankers and oligarchs have got another hero.

That is of course for a little while but doesn't time really fly.

When they're having so much fun with lie after lie after lie.

Sing a song of sixpence a pocket full of shit.

Send Diogenes amongst them his lamp would not get lit.

YOU MAKE ME FEEL

so strung

You make my knots undone
You make me feel so string has strung
And every time I see my String
I'm such a tied-up individual.

The moment that I speak
I lose the game of hide-and-seek
I don't wanna get tied up the moon
It's not just a toy balloon.

You and I are just like a couple of knots
Strolling through the meadow
Picking up lots and lots of pot

You make me feel so strung

You make me feel like my twines are undone

Hemp to be spun and a wonderful string to be strung

And even when I'm old and frayed

I'm gonna feel completed splayed

'Cause you make me feel so strung

BILL

Would you want to be a tory if you knew
the word came from thief?

Or simply grin and bear it then firmly grip your teeth.

I'm not talking about party differences to me it's all the same.

Career politicians in carpetbagger seats
they're the ones to blame.

I wonder what would have happened if
I'd forgotten to pay my tax.

Probably receive a massive fine and prison but not to relax.

But not that lot, it gets ignored till it can't be ignored any more.

Then they're thanked for their service
and simply shown the door.

Probably along with a golden handshake
a great ministerial perk.

A handshake that could be earned by us lot
in a couple of years at work.

Then I expect more sleaze will arrive about
who paid what to whom.

They all sing out loud from the songbook but
have the wrongs words for the tune.

Then I hear the popo are finally being investigated.

Internally I expect though so most of it will be truncated.

Some will no doubt have to go to win back public trust.

The shadier ones I have no illusions will again avoid the bust.

But that's how it is with an institution that investigates itself.

Leaving room for the worst of them to
continue to operate in stealth.

Sing a song a sixpence a pocket full of sticks.

They invented a legal form of lying and called it politics.

BALLS OF PAPER

Balls of screwed up paper on the writer's floor.

Balls of screwed up paper we don't see that no more.

Balls of screwed up paper in the writers bin.

Digitised homogenised now let the fun begin.

Is it really, really real without an old typewriter.

Can they say with hand on heart they really are a fighter.

With reams of wasted paper before it made the writer think.

Digitised homogenised magnetic fucking ink.

Remember the balls of paper the writer left before.

At least we now don't waste the trees we hear ecologists' roar.

Digitised homogenised cut and paste that phrase.

No balls of wasted paper like in the good old days.

However, that's another lie the good old days I mean.

Making us wish for a better world but one that has never been.

History is relative to whoever wrote it down.

You never wore a robe of silk it was just a tattered gown.

No army ever conquered and put all wrongs to right.

The truth is convoluted and black is truly white.

These days though it's different live streaming across the world.

See it as it's happening history for the
future oh so slowly unfurled.

Digitised homogenised only seconds for them to censor.

Still in control but occasionally truth
slips through the dispenser.

Digitised homogenised long gone the days of splendour.

So photographic truth is gone replaced by the great pretender.

All for one and one for all the musketeers once said.

Nowadays its selfie time and chivalry is dead.

I'll help you but first please pose with me
for my audience online.

If not good luck and my best wishes I'm sure you will be fine.

Digitised homogenised it's all just magnetic ink.

Unlike the balls of paper when a writer still had to think.

GIGGLY WATER
ZOOT POPPING

Whilst walking in the dark when I couldn't see a thing.

I trusted my instincts and the eyes of my mate String.

My advice don't look for there is nothing there to see.

I'd lead you on a winding path, well that's if you follow me.

Just waiting a moment until that time when
a moment had surely passed.

Whilst I took a sip of giggly water ready to have a blast.

So, follow me they insisted though I told
them I'd lead them astray.

No longer there to make a difference merely to laugh and play.

So off we went our merry throng.

Quite a few joined so the procession was long.

I came across a footpath I'd never noticed before.

When in that world of giggly water curiosity was the law.

It was a narrow path with overhanging
trees ready for me to explore.

So off we all went it was very dark and no-one could see a thing.

I was ok with my instincts as I said and my mate String.

It wasn't very long till somebody bumped their head.

I said, you shouldn't have followed; why not turn back instead.

But bump after bump we continued till the
end of the dark woody path.

It opened out in a street I knew so I started to proper laugh.

I told them the path has led nowhere at least
anywhere near where we're going.

The tall guy looked back at the dark woody path
with a terrible sense of knowing.

Then said he's going to give it a miss and take another route.

I decided this was time for more giggly
water and maybe a little zoot.

By this point I guess you may have started to wonder.

Although to get above you obviously must go under.

Therefore if it feels as such there's no such thing as plunder.

Was that a trip down Thesaurus Street or
merely a massive blunder.

Was there a point to this blah, blah, blah? Yes at least to me.

I said, I'd lead them on a winding path
that's if they followed…see?

So off we all went back the way we had come.

Except the tall bloke and two of his chums.

We then had to cross the railway line.

Well, we didn't it was just an idea of mine.

Then clambered across a deep ploughed
field everyone got very muddy.

Homoconsumerus at their best a future anthropology study.

They spotted a light straight ahead and asked if that is the party.

I told them it's just a red flashing light they
were bound to be a lot more arty.

But nevertheless, they went that way I took a different route.

When they realised their mistake, I was waiting smoking a zoot.

Off we went again up past a strawberry farm.

Still in the rightish direction so it couldn't do no harm.

Then a fence of barbed wire blocked our route.

I wandered off for a piss and lit another zoot.

I saw the place where the barbed wire came to an end.

So I thought I'd go and tell them all but
I'm not quite round the bend.

I never went back I went forward on the other side of the wire.

When I got back to where my entourage were
a couple were still climbing higher.

This seemed like a good place to make another zoot.

I was getting vibrations from my hobnail suit.

It felt like I had popping candy in my head which
was weird because I know I'm sane.

So I wondered if perhaps the giggly water
had somehow melted my brain.

But no, I was sitting under a pylon and it had started to rain.

Plenty of time to enjoy the sensation before setting off again.

Then a trundle through the woods down to a stream I know.

It didn't matter how seemingly ridiculous
wherever I went they would go.

Eventually after my ramble I set about my original task.

If at anytime they had wanted directions they merely had to ask.

Because some of them were moaning now
I very soon became bored.

Finally leading them to the rave this
pilgrimage had a just reward.

HUMMUS AND FALAFELS

Hummus and Falafels although they are very nice.

Quickly become as boring as good old plain boiled rice.

When you go out for lunch and its all you can get.

They do cater for vegans but not that well yet.

With fifteen main meal options surely more could be.

Not another plate of corpses that have no appeal to me.

It has always been this way I've seen this shit for years.

So, vegans still get marginalised and can't
go and eat with their peers.

Unless they care to go to the usual fast-food place.

It's possible to buy some food that never had a face.

Those that do go into one and live to tell the tale.

Of people sitting eating corpses on quite an epic scale.

I couldn't even enter one now because of the smell of death.

I went in once decades ago and couldn't catch my breath.

Obviously, there are some better than others.

But for me when entering the smell of death smothers.

Any hunger that I might have had has very quickly gone.

I know that some are trying so why's it so terribly wrong.

I'm know it is getting better that is very plain to see.

But hummus and falafels though very
nice is all they're offering me.

I AN I

So, I got back from the hospital and couldn't
replace most of my rings.

Mostly because I'm blind as a bat and
wonky among other things.

So, my bestie Natasha came round to help
and got most of the blighters in.

Not the balls though, they need to be bigger
not as small as the head of a pin.

The daith and conch had started to scab in not much over a day.

Which makes perfect sense, to both of me,
as they used to love to say.

They've both been quiet for ages now, so
I wonder what is brewing.

Oh yeah, even though they are a part of of me
I have no idea what they're doing.

That's just like what's happening to our
country although maybe less severe.

Well this is Britain in crisis nearly everyone cowering in fear.

That's almost a metaphor, yes almost, but yet not quite.

As it's hypothetical psychology as opposed to an actual fight.

People are shitting themselves about the cost of living.

As usual the government aren't even one shit giving.

Watch this space be back soon the shelves continue to say.

Whilst out hunting for essentials more and more each day.

Look at how prices are rising? An old lady said to me.

As she stretched up to reach a packet they
had the audacity to label tea.

I think it's just human history repeating itself once again.

There once was a war to end all wars it didn't, that much is plain.

It's a great way to get rid of the masses
with honour on a battlefield.

With life not much better for those left
behind history has revealed.

The world economy had completely changed.

Stocks and shares were all very strange.

Ordinary folks using ordinary cash.

Didn't understand the stock market crash.

That it led to the great depression there in the United States.

People were literally starving there
nothing to put on their plates.

No matter where you went there was no work to be found.

It started in America as I said but travelled the world around.

This great depression as it was called though
not so great for the masses.

World leaders very sticky people this time like winter molasses.

The knock-on effect worldwide, ended with world war two.

The factories were there the workers and raw materials too.

The factories all re-opened; I find that odd don't you?

So logically then they could have always been so.

But I'm just a benderskum so what would I know.

That got rid of loads of us but still not enough so it seems.

Which only begs the question; about, androids
and electric sheep dreams?

Covid deaths so far about six and three quarters of a million.

I guess there are still too many of us; can our
world sustain another billion?

Well of course it could unfortunately though
there's a human habit to beat.

A habit of consuming chopped up corpses
as if that's a nice thing to eat.

So now we are seeing water as the new economy.

Water not fit for drinking is currently what's bothering me.

Whatever comes out of your kitchen tap
is likely polluted with shit.

Which they're also dumping in the rivers
and sea and not just a little bit.

You realise this is just my opinion a benderskum point of view.

A load of the treacle in this sticky world
I'm slowly wading through.

Recently two old friends of mine that had never previously met.

Both saying I've heard of you before but
meeting until now not yet.

They live such separate lives it was very unlikely indeed.

The hand of fate intervened that's a force that always succeeds.

Abbi said hi I'm Abbi and as far as I know she is.

Mad Dennis said I'm Mad Dennis. Honestly
I'm not taking the piss.

He's a something or other physicist so
could make a fat loadabuck.

Finally accepting his place in the world looking
proper mad scientist as fuck.

But not everyone runs for money there are so much better ways.

To have a load of jolly not lolly to while away the days.

Chatting to Abbi, was Michael and he is Mad Dennis' son.

If Mad Dennis was actually a Guru, he
could be 'The Chosen One'.

Those two were talking hierarchies and
other psychological babble.

They'd have been better off playing guitars or
backgammon, chess or scrabble.

Sing a song a sixpence a pocket full of politicians.

If you emptied that into the sea you'd be
fined for toxic emissions.

Unlike all those water companies that are poisoning our coasts.

Bad Escherichia coli on every beach human waste the host.

I think I'm stopping writing this to cook myself some food.

I won't eat it in until I go stop writing I'm
horrible but still not that rude.

IN THE LAND OF IN-BETWEEN

Greetings to all you revellers in the land of in-between.

Festivities land I'm talking about the glittery Halloween.

I'm luckily marked safe from it all and expected to be alone.

My friend came round on Christmas Eve
for the charger for her phone.

Anana incidentally is bananas longest palindromic substring.

I know that's nothing to do with it but still
thought worth mentioning.

Her visit was no drama at all with me oh its
benderskum here not String.

He's asleep in his cupboard as he sleeps standing up.

Him and Genevieve went clubbing so I won't interrupt.

Vienna last night, caught the red eye this morning.

While I was asleep still long before dawning.

Hitched in a taxi from the airport all the way to here.

I suppose that being invisible makes things very clear.

The logistics of which I can't even imagine.

But being a hacker that is Genevieve's passion.

So Genevieve does all the clickety clicks.

Arranging stuff to keep their life full of ticks.

I've not seen much of Glynn the hunchback
except at breakfast time.

Walter popped up the other day his muscles are in sad decline.

He keeps a stock of energy drinks hidden in the pantry of doom.

Silly man thinks it's a secret from us the
oddly sweet foolish buffoon.

Olly though I haven't seen but he's definitely been about.

He left behind a trail that was him without a doubt.

Half eaten gingerbread people everywhere he goes.

Where they all have come from goodness only knows.

But there they all are nevertheless.

If I didn't eat them they'd become quite a mess.

They recently became my staple diet.

They are honestly tasty you really should try it.

Not that I've ever eaten staples, that'd be too stupid even for me.

But gingerbread people go really well with a lovely cup of tea.

Did you see him when he made that no snow poem?

He was visible then but you'd still never know him.

When he said the heating's on full with
the doors and windows open.

I didn't let him actually do it and he was actually only joking.

He's not always invisible but the mask you get to see.

Is a proper bit of genius tech and nothing to do with me.

He appears to be wearing an anonymous mask.

If you've not seen him keep an eye out that is a worthy task.

He has a tech gadget that automatically detects.

If you try to record and immediately reflects.

If an attempt is made to videogle or photomagraph him.

It has to be one of those methods as he is merely an antonym.

Ordinary cameras or other devices like
you know, camera phones.

Only take photos like x-rays so all you see is bones.

So you can't take his picture, now that is clever stuff.

While the big bad wolf continues to huff and puff.

Anyway, back to the festivities in this season of good cheer.

I could say it was fucking amazing but would I be being sincere.

I don't mind the company but equally happy to be on my own.

I'm never actually lonely though I spend lots of time alone.

Even if you're with people they're often glued to their phones.

This friend however in my opinion didn't want to be alone.

It meant I had to change my plans for my
two day old leftover stew.

So that and some veggie sausages and potato waffles too.

Cordon vert however though not worthy of a diploma.

With a tin of tomatoes, it was proper nice
no sign of an Xmas food coma.

So, this weekend is another one this one with fireworks galore.

I think I'm likely to stay inside enjoy hibernation some more.

I hope that not too many animals get distressed.

But happy New year to all and I know I once more digressed.

So sing a song a sixpence a pocket full of air.

Writing this took me ages but I bet you just don't care.

ZANGLOID

poetry

...

It appeared that Vogon poetry was making
my nephew's head hurt

Although not Vogon but Zangloid though
obviously just as splurt

I have come to realise how selfish it is to keep it to myself

So, I took a book of Zangloid Poetry down
from my invisible shelf

So here for your reading pleasure a most beautiful short extract

Though it's won't be to everyone's taste that is a cast iron fact

...

Where drurglespleens come frangling the best bufoogly sparks

Though pargricks klep ponglows fonk
and furglies pinnt and vark

Barge verdannga boobop belay the frangling now

Pass de bookah boobop yogi kelp ponglows chiao

As if a kargle blent its steeg enveloping furglies pinnt

Epicurateoslushily the demanga toot et mintt

Perging furbees ponka nests eases yogi floomers

Panglefak badeebly squint according to the rumours

...

To be fair that last line in honesty was a little bit guessed

It's translated from ancient alien scrolls but I did my level best

KIND TO ANIMALS

Am I a vegan or is that just a label?

I'm kind to animals as much as I'm able.

Am I a vegan or an average Joe?

I am just a benderskum possibly why I don't know?

Although folks assume it so decide that's what I am.

They can think what they like, I don't give a damn.

No I'm totally kind to animals which is
something you may have heard.

I try not to harm a living being and vegan is merely a word.

If you say 'kind to animals' instead of vegan, you may find.

Becoming 'kind to animals' could soon be on your mind.

Just say I'm

'kind to animals'

say it again, repeat.

Or,

I'd like to be 'kind to animals'

but I couldn't give up meat.

Or leather shoes or handbags and fashion.

Or cheese, milk, eggs or honey whatever is my passion.

Everything you need can be harvested from a plant.

You'd like to be 'kind to animals'

but you simply can't.

LEGALISEDISH

On the 1st of November 2018 cannabis was legalised.

For certain medical conditions prohibitions new disguise.

I asked a canna pharmacist quite expecting this reply.

As many it seems are totally unaware truly no word of a lie.

The difference between this legal marijuana
to that other evil pot.

He replied is nothing whatsoever a difference they have not.

But the moment of transformation is the moment it is sealed.

In our super magic containers where its
healing effects are revealed.

Before it goes into them it is still at schedule one.

Meaning as for medicinal properties it has absolutely none.

Presumably everyone nowadays knows
that simply isn't the truth.

If you didn't look at the difference if you need to see some proof.

The difference between legal and illegal just in case you forgot.

Is one has been placed by a pharmacist in a transformation pot.

The war on drugs is ideological and has no moral basis.

Whereas cannabis in our daily lives can lead to homeostasis.

So, when someone goes to prison for donating cannabis oil.

To people that are very ill, it makes my blood proper boil.

A NEW SPIV?

Another bowl of right-wing political stew.

So what does that mean for the likes of me and you?

More robbing the poor to give to the rich.

Maybe Dennis Moore wasn't a silly bitch.

Like they claimed in a Monty Python episode.

Dennis wanted lupins this lot might explode.

Leader out, leader in, leader out, leader in.

Leader out again making our heads proper spin.

Will this one be for better or for worse?

Tightening up outgoings from the public purse.

Cutting services and slimming down of spending.

Austerity two is here patent no longer pending.

Reducing the payments to the already loaded.

Who'll pick up the pieces after it's exploded.

Once again, they'll have to borrow more loot.

From the unknown banker in its invisibility suit.

There's a new spiv in town in good old drowning street.

After a hopeful opponent bowed its head in defeat.

Will the new one be any different to what there was before?

I think it's most unlikely they're all rotten to the core.

Whatsit Thatcher yeah you know the name.

Bliar and Camayron different but the same.

Since 1979 the only prime ministers elected as such.

Although of course politically really not so much.

When they first took over the role is what I'm on about.

All the others arrived when their predecessor was booted out.

Greyjor, brown, mayhem, bojo and truss.

Some of them no doubt wasted money on a battle bus.

Private jets to fly them around but this I think is preposterous.

Flying wherever they wish to go including
to climate conference.

I wish they had an ounce of decorum.

Instead of being the usual oxymoron.

The new spiv claimed to be different it
really was time for change.

Then reappoints a monster so why does that not seem strange.

Will they still allow fracking? You never can really tell.

If they think it makes money they'll certainly open the well.

The one that made the earthquake before the moratorium.

The plans for fracking should go up in smoke
but not like a crematorium.

Don't bother to listen to me at all I'm considered a bit bohemian.

Just watch what they get up to you'll notice
integrity is far from premium.

Still allowing the richest here to say they live abroad.

Whilst remaining here all the time why is that not fraud.

In 1987 for not paying taxes a famous jockey was jailed.

It was once illegal to not pay your tax but
that ship has long since sailed.

Unless you're just the average person on the street.

So therefore, not a part of the so called elite.

Or even one of the great pretenders.

Other people's money spenders.

The Cayman Islands is one place they hide their dirty money.

The governments are nothing but gangsters
it's a joke but just not funny.

The other lot are no better trying to remove the left leaners.

Eventually emerging with right with us lot sent to the cleaners.

They want to ban protest completely, so
you need to listen to this.

They can electronically tag you for attending

and I'm not taking the piss.

If you've been to a protest in the last five years or so.

They can do that to you I'll have you know.

There's a monster out there having vile wet dreams.

She has a pleasant enough face but she's worse than she seems.

So, if you're thought as a problem you'll
be on some dodgy watch list.

They do make it up as they go along maybe
something else that gets missed.

So how does this bode for the future will all our rights be gone.

It seems to be heading in that direction and
I really hope that I'm wrong.

I hear talk of revolution though I don't think it will be the thing.

But something needs doing and quickly or
the fat lady will start to sing.

Maybe just a poem or song could be seen as a riotous act.

That which is merely hearsay now tomorrow could be fact.

NEW WEIRD ORDER

a corona fable

Remember when the pubs reopened no
longer just gardens at least?

Inside it was previously scary because
there lurked corona-beast.

Inside unless you were seated you still needed to wear a mask.

Which didn't really make much, sense so
here's what they said if you asked.

It can get you when you're standing or
moving from table to table.

But seated you are safe then the story became a fable.

Nail salons, Libraries and community centres too.

Theme parks, Drive-ins and finally at last the zoo.

You could even get your haircut then go to the village fete.

This may have all caused a third wave but by
then it would've been too late.

If you were getting married you couldn't have many guests.

Or the popo would come calling to declare you corona-pests.

If you lived in a care home you could nominate two visitors.

As they say no-one expected the Spanish fucking inquisisitors.

Well that was how it was before but things have changed a lot.

To put it in perspective the country had gone to pot.

Though not the sort of pot that you could even smoke.

A different pot completely another corona-joke.

They said the jab would not protect you from the disease.

But a shiny vaxxy passport would bring it to its knees.

So back to all the venues that opened for us all to use.

Bubbles meeting bubbles so much for people to choose.

But if you wanted to travel to another cunt aree.

The test for that cost an arm and a leg because

simply nothing is for free.

You could go and get some exercise in an indoor sports facility.

To try and lose your corona-belly caused by immobility.

Many still wanted to go abroad in spite
of the locked down borders.

They created a world of me, me, me,
welcome to the new weird order.

NEVER WRITTEN
A POEM

I've never written a poem the poems however wrote me.

Even the one with my Ontzichtbare vriend
that says toedeledokie.

There's nothing I can do I guess that is just their fate.

Even if engraved on a fire guard you wouldn't call them grate.

If you try to make sense of the world trust me give it a miss.

If everything is pre-ordained someone is taking the piss.

But do I even believe 'That'? Well, 'That' remains to be seen.

Though I'd been to London many times I
never believed in the queen.

Or any other member of the so-called upper class.

On its voyage to join NATO the UK flagship set sail.

Not thwarted by iceberg or cyclone or gale.

It sailed out of Portsmouth near the Isle of White.

Then it broke down a three billion pounds pile of shite.

It must be saving tons of fuel simply by breaking down.

I bet all the admirals are tearing their hair
out in good old Pompous town.

Three billion for an aircraft carrier thirty-
seven for a mobile app.

That's forty billion in one foul swoop what a pile of crap.

Money really well spent you never heard anyone say.

If you're a pal of the leaders, it's always a good payday.

There isn't an energy crisis I doubt you'd have disagreed.

If you knew how much profit these companies
make you'd know it's a crisis of greed.

NO SNOW

Why do you all think it's snowing, I mean
that's a thing of the past?
These days we have slush puppy rain so it's never gonna last.
I keep getting sent these pictures of everything covered in snow.
They are obviously fake I guess you think I don't know.
Snow isn't real it's just in your mind.
I think you're deluded and that's me being kind.
I know you believe that it's cold you can feel.
And the white fluffy blobs from the sky are real.
I believe that it's mass hypnosis but please rest assured.
I believe the mass hypnotists are likely to soon get bored.
All back to blah, blah, blah normal and
forget about snow once again.
We'll get back our British weather once more
have lovely drizzle and rain.
Snowdrops from the sky are real you tell me,
and this is just me being kind.
You're all in need of rubber rooms because
you're obviously out of your minds.

Galanthus byzantinus is a snowdrop however it still isn't snow.
But a tiny white flower endemic to Istanbul,
I thought you'd like to know.
Not the snowdrop we find here growing in the spring.
Ours is called Galanthus nivalis but here's a funny thing.
Byzantinus comes from Turkey but not even called Delight.
And if you bother to fact check poems you
may find that some fact is right.
This type of snowdrop is different you can't roll them into a ball.
And if you made a big pile of them it
wouldn't be a snowman at all.
So prove to me that snow exists and don't
say it falls from the sky.
Because my dears like chicken licken it
was another government lie.
Don't bother to show me videos I've heard of special effects.
And as if I've not heard of photoshop do you
think I'm Tyrannosaurus Rex?

So off with you now and your silly idea that
snow is a thing that exists.
You'll be telling me next you buy what you
like from the oligopolists.
But that is entirely beside the point maybe it's in the air.
You all seem to believe that snow exists
and are seeing it everywhere.
I know you truly believe in snow and possibly that I'm insane.

Why would the government make it up?
I've heard again and again.
Fuel prices rise on demand sometimes with more than a swing.
So if everyone thinks its snowy and cold its
kerching, kerching, and kerching.

NO SNOWLIGARCH

a poem by Olly

The fact I am an oligarch becomes evidentially clear.

My central heating is on full blast don't be surprised to hear.

Doors and windows all open wide to drive away the bitter cold.

Imaginary snow can't land near my home
so don't say you've not been told.

Rain is fine however because I know that it is real.

But frozen little fluffy balls, perleaze that has no appeal.

Now people are trying to claim it's snowing in their city.

I could put something funny here but I'm simply not that witty.

They are sending photos to prove I will tell them simply stop.

I've been on your planet long enough to
have heard of photoshop.

So just to be quite straight because you all deserve to know.

You are under mass hypnosis and there's no such thing as snow.

I know it formerly existed I remember
seeing it when I was a kid.

The cold white stuff was everywhere so I
stayed in the warm and hid.

MATHS

There's trouble at mill Monty Python once said.

There's trouble everywhere from what I just read.

So, what is the answer from the Westmonster psychopaths.

Everyone up to the age of 18 must do plenty more maths.

I guess that's what happens with a financier as Prime Minister.

If I want to make up a conspiracy theory, it
could be something far more sinister.

The doors have been opened since democracy was broken.

Anything good they say they'll do is fake or merely a token.

Hospital trusts running food banks to
make sure the staff can eat.

A monster says budget better in the usual arrogant tweet.

When they sold off the country's assets
the cleverest of soothsayers.

Couldn't have foreseen it still being subsidised by taxpayers.

The worst of that funding is it's to make
the shareholders bigger profits.

In a world that's turned into a shop there
seems no way to stop it.

They've been making things increasingly
worse year after year after year.

Nothing has changed for the better in this constant state of fear.

Now it has turned full circle again with the
threat of another world war.

I thought we had learned from history never to open that door.

I guess we have but this time it's a different
because it's televised.

Although it can still be edited it's much
harder when it's broadcast live.

Just something to hide behind which will cover up the truth.

But I don't believe a word of it I'm much too long in the tooth.

Are they really that inept or trying to run the country down?

Before the people finally wake up and chase them out of town.

They still blame the ones that were there before.

When actually that was twelve years ago or more.

What we need is a different system not this
antiquated first past the post.

What we have isn't representative of us at
best it's democracy's ghost.

GETTING TATTOOED

If I feel like inking up my body it heals very quickly, well mostly though Graft Versus Host disease has a go sometimes. I'm lucky I've got weird skin because of my double DNA my immune system is super efficient in some regards as it's only just over eight years old.

That's due to the female DNA in my bone marrow so consequently my blood; as it's where blood is made and well the immune system is part of the blood system. So, damage like tattooing heal super quick and tend not to scab.

However also because my immune system is super efficient and female it doesn't recognise any of the bits that were here before, my whole body particularly my organs, which of course includes skin because they have male DNA.

Although in normal circumstances every cell in our bodies is renewed over a seven year period and even with not so normal circumstances like having a bone marrow transplant, if the chimera thing didn't happen, after seven years the new male if male and female if female immune system would become part of the whole. A bone marrow transplant is literally stem cells harvested from a donor that had hormone boosters to make them produce the stem cells which were then harvested by a system pretty much like kidney dialysis where the blood is pumped our cleaned and extra stem cells harvested because of course we make them all the time they are part of the immune system, blah, blah, blah.

In my case however it's not so the stem cells that arrived at my bone marrow found nothing but dead cells which sometimes happen and had nothing to replicate from so reverted back to the donor DNA from remnants in the transfusion it seems so made my new bone marrow female, so my blood and particularly organs will never match.

So, as I said damaging myself i.e. tattoos heal quickly because my immune system wants me not to be broken, simultaneously continually trying to break me. My diagnosis as a doctor of garbology is I have a schizophrenic immune system. Lucky I live in this bad cartoon then I suppose.

NON SMOKER

Arriving at Amsterdam Centraal with
that feeling of being home.

I thought of what they say about Romans
even though I wasn't in Rome.

So walking out of the station on my way to town.

Saw a guy sat begging looking proper down.

I knew that he was English the moment that he spoke.

He asked me for a shag in really bad Dutch so then I had to joke.

Sorry mate you're not my type I just don't fancy you.

He then tried to explain it further till he realised I already knew.

I gave him my nearly full pouch of Drum,
skins and a lighter as well.

Plus, twenty euros to buy food or whatever he
hugged me but eeuww what a smell.

I suggested to have luck getting shags in
future first try to get a shower.

Because after getting close I know you don't
smell fuck all like a flower.

Then I wandered to the hotel to dump my heavy bag.

Amusing myself remembering the homeless

guy and his request for a shag.

I then went to buy a new pouch in my regular tobacco store.

On my way back out I shouted out loudly
and this is what I swore.

You stupid cunt why did you buy more shag?
Because you no longer smoke.

The shopkeeper looked at me angrily I said sorry private joke.

He wanted to know what it was that made me such a joker.

I told him that even though I bought tobacco
it appears I'm not a smoker.

What do you mean? He asked me so I then tried to explain.

He then told me get out of my shop you English are all insane.

It was probably the mention of String, you
know my invisible friend.

He's real but just invisible, not imaginary,
I'm not round the bend.

I did still smoke of course smelly green
stuff that's rolled into a zoot.

In places that were formerly known as houses of ill repute.

Although of course these days they are accepted as normality.

Shame that here in blighty the law has
reefer madness mentality.

Nowadays though I don't smoke at all my
lungs are proper broken.

I've had pneumonia a time or three of which I may have spoken.

I still vape a bit if I need a quick hit of nature's best pain reliever.

If you believe that wouldn't work you've

listened to the great deceiver.

Prohibition is its name and the mother of organised crime.

Organised crime is a modern-day menace
born in an earlier time.

The first major act of prohibition that had
a worldwide domino effect.

Gave small criminal gangs a product and
a reason to interconnect.

The government of America banned alcohol
supposedly for everyone's health.

However, the real reason was the promotion of oil
and to bolster some rich people's wealth.

Up till then if you actually drove a car.

Your fuel often came in a liquor jar.

With alcohol getting banned petrol cars were urgently needed.

So DuPont opened General Motors and
the oil industry succeeded.

Leaving engines that still used alcohol difficult to run.

Another way for the newly organised gangs to make funds.

Eventually of course the gangs got so rich.

They did what they liked with barely a hitch.

Then became invisible but there in plain sight.

Robbing us all 24/7 instead of just at night.

Anyway, enough of that blah, blah, blah
I have plenty more, believe.

Doesn't that leave wondering? What's the
government got up its sleeve?

Maar nu kruipt de aap uit de mouw, om jou te beroven.

And if you didn't get the gist of that at all
they'll probably turn you over.

BLAH, BLAH, BLAH

I joined a group on social media I'm not entirely sure why.

Maybe it was out of interest but possibly because I was high.

A state that's nice to be in as it alleviates my pain.

And when the hurt takes over, I just get high again.

I even stood for parliament something
you may not have known.

I stood for the rights of all marijuana users
and to legally grow my own.

Growing the plant is illegal a fact I can't deny.

Home grown has no medicinal value is another filthy lie.

After legalising in 2018 new clinics opened.

Proving that the drug laws are dated and broken.

They are now permitted to prescribe legal oil and herb.

So, keeping homegrown at schedule one
is ideological and absurd.

It makes interaction with the police even
worse than it was before.

As most of them are still unaware of the changes in the law.

They often still think it's illegal when
you show them your script.

Believing you made it in photoshop and if you
argue with them, you're nicked.

It isn't allowed on some social media to
show pictures of your nugs.

Because the algorithm has already decided
the picture is dangerous drugs.

Marijuana, weed, ganja, cannabis, herb or pot.

Many names it goes by but dangerous drug it's not.

On the oxymoron called social media you may not be aware.

If the algorithm doesn't like your message,
it will not let you share.

In fact, you may get banned metaphorically shown the door.

There is a carefully hidden agenda of this you can be sure.

Be aware that if they don't like what you have to say.

They'll delete your account and wipe you away.

Click you're on... Yes, but click you're gone.

Social media is always like this a very modern curse.

Unlike printed media for nonfiction or story or verse.

Although these days it seems really old books are the target.

They want to censor everything for the
homogenised digital market.

It makes me wonder about the bible and
the content found therein.

If they looked at the book of Leviticus it'll
probable make their heads start to spin.

But keep on writing articles and the truth will filter out.

They try to silence us out in the street but

still we continued to shout.

My message is very simple give me what's mine by right.

That's what they don't want and bluntly
refuse so still I continue my fight.

I want to legally reap what I've sewn.

My Human right is to Grow My Own.

I truly believe in lawful because legal just is not true.

But because it's there it makes me swear if
you enforce it then Fuck You.

You might think I'm just an old pothead and
I can't really say it's not true.

But believe me from the bottom of my heart I wouldn't wish my pain on you.

HISTORY WHO'S STORY?

I'm here to tell you a story in my classical poetry style.

About some prohibitionists all of whom I think were vile.

Although classical style is a stretch of
reality as you will quickly see.

But the second line is the honest truth I think you might agree.

It started with a newsman and politician
name of William Hearst.

Eventually joined by others but he was one of the first.

He owned a lot of newspapers and forests to make paper with.

He appeared like an honest businessman but acted like a spiv.

He invented yellow journalism to make his papers sell.

So instead of news there was fiction and

it made the president yell.

'When I open up my paper to read all of the news,

I want to read the facts of it not some journalistic views'

He'd held that view for a while and Hearst
he was known to deplore.

He blamed yellow journalism for helping stir
up the Spanish-American war.

The president's name was Theodore he
expanded National Parks.

Lots of the land owned by William Hearst,
Ted's bite was as bad as his bark.

So, Hearst could not cut down those particular
trees en masse to run his paper mills.

But he owned eighty Thousand acres of forestry
in Mexico which was part of America still.

So, he set off to Mexico to cut down acres of
trees with his usual ornery gang.

They were stopped in their tracks by Pancho
Villa's crew and thwarted in their plan.

Mexico at this time was annexed to the US of
A but negotiating independence.

The President had pardoned all bandit gangs
to give himself ascendance.

Pancho Villa's bandit gang was the majority
of the northern division.

Their battle song *La Cucaracha* caused Hearst's men indecision.

They sang of Marijuana of which Hearst's men had never heard.

So, Hearst vilified Marijuana and Mexicans
to which other racists concurred.

This went on for many years he was joined of course by others.

Many it seemed had similar views about our
brown skinned sisters and brothers.

Andrew Mellon oft overlooked was the US
Treasury Secretary of state.

An investment banker in fossil views so the
hemp industry was something to hate.

He made his niece's husband head of the
Federal Bureau of Narcotics.

A racist guy named Anslinger who claimed
marijuana made people psychotic.

Who then employed an expert on drugs the
specialist Doctor James Munch.

A scientist who to put it plainly, was completely out to lunch.

He claimed in court and this is a fact.

Smoking Marijuana turned him into a bat.

Or at least to put another way in order to explain.

After that he told marijuana had made him temporarily insane.

Back to Mellon had investments with
Lamott DuPont the second.

To build cars that run on fossil fuels the
age of petroleum beckoned.

Any colour you want a long as its black at
the birth of General Motors.

Along with investments from John D Rockefeller
and some other fossil oil promoters.

Between them they lobbied to make growing too
expensive for even the richest hemp farmer.

The Rockefeller's had all the herbalist closed down
in favour of their petrochemical Pharma.

With the Marijuana Tax act firmly entrenched in the law.

They lobbied the world to follow their path
but greed was what it was for.

Over the years activists have tried to make
governments to see their mistake.

But here in the UK it seems obvious to me why
the initiative is so hard to take.

Those here invested in the cannabis industry.

Would lose a lot of profit if they make our actions free.

So, what is the hold up and who is to blame?

Corporations or Government, or are they one and the same?

OLLY GARK'S RANT

Hello again sports fans remember me a lizard overlord.

I thought I'd add my bit in here to be fair I was getting bored.

Not being from here I arrived aeons ago
and I've kept an eye on you lot.

Are you actually crazy as a species or have you just lost the plot.

When we came here our intention was eating the lot of you.

Eventually there were too many humans to go into the stew.

It was then decided to change our cuisine
become a tad more choosy.

So off we all went to the decision room
you'd probably call the Jacuzzi.

Nowadays we don't just eat any of you
as we veganally specialise.

Of course, to taste the very best corn fed vegans are the prize.

However even though your populations are
almost completely free range.

They are almost impossible not to find because

the rest of you think they're strange.

We've noticed of late a lot of you seem
to believe you are actually free.

Well let me tell you, you are free range but still belong to me.

When I say me I really mean us lot, we're many just as we're one.

But I digress which always happens when
I'm having so much fun.

Have you seen our latest puppet it's the
funniest we've put there yet.

Will it last more than two years I wouldn't suggest you bet.

It will obviously make things so much worse
for you lot I mean the majority.

They will likely cause an uprising as it
tries to assert its authority.

Surrounded by nothing but its diabolically clueless mates.

Having a jolly in the restaurant with their
overstuffed subsidised plates.

Whilst you lot of course have nothing but
your disgusting maccy dees.

Two all beef patty, special blah, blah, blah

perleeze.

In Britain they are not top food supplier
and this you may not know.

There are nearly twice as many foodbanks
an industry on the grow.

Oh is that the time I'd better be off, take care, toodaloo.

Did I really say take care? Apologies, I meant

Fuck You

ODE TO A LETTUCE

My goodness your former leader really was the worst.

It cracked me up so much I thought my lungs would burst.

And my face nearly cracked from my endless grin.

Who knew it'd be so much fun when we put it in.

It blamed everything on Putin but if it only knew.

He's actually one of us yes, he's an Oligarch too.

Or to be precise one of your overlord owners.

Not in the slightest bit grateful to anything from you donors.

Anyway, back to mistrust and what it was telling it's fans.

With its awful squawking voice and waving pointless hands.

Talking about an anti-growth coalition
spreading anti-growth lies.

Not even vaguely trying to grow some imaginary pies.

It was our social experiment the neo-liberal worm.

Put there to make you lot toe the line and
hopefully...well, squirm.

Hoping to cut the benefits to the sick and disabled.

Also, the poor, old, vulnerable or anyone similarly labelled.

It stole from the poor to give to the rich.

Such fun to watch it pouncing without the slightest hitch.

What else did it get up to it wanted to bring back fracking.

What a waste of time and resources for that it had our backing.

It'll make your water burn with gases destroying your planet.

We don't care we're farming you, did you think we didn't plan it?

Anyway, the news of late was all a huge distraction.

While telling you all you're fucked, you're
screwed to see if we get a reaction.

Toedeledoki

HEMPLIFE

a poem in a poem

Sitting on the floor inside my front door
after my groceries arrive.

I emptied all the baskets out, watched by the delivery guy.

Waiting patiently.

I have to sit not stand to do this it's too ouchy for my body.

I'm often in a state of zero energy which I
personally find proper shoddy.

Excess gravity.

Wondering at my groceries all sprawled across the floor.

Looking and for a moment thinking what did I buy it all for.

Am I fucking crazy?

Lying in a heap ready to be put away in its place.

You'd notice I wasn't smiling if you could see my face.

Maybe not, maybe.

Sometimes becoming a rare moment of despair for me.

It wasn't like this before they took a deposit see.

I didn't mind paying.

Some places still deliver in carriers and take 10p deposit.

You know the ocean is already full of plastic shit.

I'm just saying.

Even paper bags aren't much better, resources are short.

Recycling is great but there's so much more to be taught.

And also, to learn.

Recycling is limited although not just a waste of time.

To say that is ridiculous to do it a start but not nearly sublime.

Everything in turn.

Hemp however is very sustainable in oh so many ways.

If I listed even half of them your mind would be in a haze.

Ooh a bit like pot.

Paper, plastics, oils an abundance of potential uses.

Why don't we use it more apart from all the excuses?

Or maybe not.

Corporate greed and racist creed have lead us to where are now.

The field of narrative is barren and needing
much more than a plough.

A new way of doing stuff.

Particle boards that are stronger than wood.

Oils from the seeds that are known to be good.

Not just having a puff.

An acre of hemp can produce 300 gallons of oil.

A process that leaves 6,000lbs of nutritious flour as spoil.

Who knew?

The stalks and the hurds can be used for
so many thousand things.

The reason they aren't is fossil fuel lobbyists
pulling the governments strings.

Not you.

You first need a licence to grow it something
you may not have known.

Rapeseed, Barley, oats, etc; there's no
license for them to be grown.

How strange.

Food, clothing, shelter, fuel, etc produced
from growing one plant.

Give me one good reason then why they simply aren't.

Nothing's changed.

I guess that way outbalances my momentary down.

Even if it makes me grimace or worse still even frown.

If just for a while.

However, life is way too special and precious a condition.

To worry for less than an instant so I'll
stop that without a petition.

And yet I smile.

PEACE

I couldn't help but notice back in Christmas week.

A time when love and kindness was apparently at its peak.

Peace and goodwill to everyone I'm sure I heard them speak.

Unfortunately, it's not for everyone for
some the prospects were bleak.

Not that I'm a humbug I wished you all my best.

To enjoy your annual festivities and all the fucking rest.

Then when it was done and dusted a time
for New Year's resolutions.

Did you consider the state the world is in
and try to think of solutions.

There are many things that are simply not
right that's how I think and feel.

If you didn't want things to be better for all
your Christmas spirit wasn't real.

PLANT BASED

isn't the same as vegan

Suddenly it seems plant-based vegans abound.

They are making corporations a very pretty pound.

Although this won't be popular it's unlikely to cause a riot.

Vegan is a way of life while plant based is just a diet.

So, the people at the top.

Altered what's in the shop.

Plant based foods galore.

However, a few things more.

Extra added ingredients.

Not for your convenience.

Quorn is vile I have to say.

80% of its RNA.

Needs removing to make it edible.

A fact I find totally incredible.

Faky baky plant-based meat.

Fabulous food for the apologists to eat.

A different poison on a different plate.

While the shops make profit at a higher rate.

Plant based burgers that seem to bleed.

A new agenda for corporate greed.

Don't just eat any old plant-based meat loads of it is disgusting.

If you really believe it's all healthy, you're
obviously very trusting.

The Westminster psychopaths once again
have turned their back on the needy.

While stuffing their faces in parliament because
they are much, much more than greedy.

They give themselves a pay rise because
it's what they really need.

It takes a special person with a special sort of greed.

Monty Python summed them up with
the character Mr. Creosote.

They stuff their faces all day long until their bellies bloat.

They don't give a toss when children starve
in fact they probably gloat.

But there is a way to put this right.

An end to the government's greedy shite.

The government do not care about us and
think they are being shrewd.

Thinking that they have fooled us all they
are extremely fucking rude.

Resource based economy is the way of the future.

An old new way much more effective than a suture.

Don't be fooled grow your food.

In the ground life renewed.

Plant a seed, watch it grow and before long you'll have. food

Without adding to the bank balance of
the extremely fucking rude.

POINTLESS

Do recognise this? And I'm not just taking the piss.

Honestly, I'm not joking it isn't fun that I'm poking.

Just my commenting on a system that's clearly broken.

The masses carefully listen, but after the leader has spoken.

There's no solace to be found.

None of that sacred middle ground.

Not even a hint of any compromise.

Just another pile of political lies.

Or if you want be to be blunt.

Because I'm a proper mouthy…bloke.

Did I say it wasn't fun I poke?

Well what if I said that what I said was merely a mirror image?

And then suggest because it rhymes we
play a game of scrimmage.

Rhyming just for the sake of it really annoys poets I've seen.

The reason I'm doing it here is to be poetically mean.

Anyway, before I digress further still and
lose my track completely.

Oh no too late there was a point but what it was defeats me.

It's ok though nonsense really has no true direction.

It's all perhaps misleading merely another complete deflection.

Word masturbation for the want of a better.

Mounting excitement with every single letter.

One finger typing it's taking far too long.

There's the point again, on no my bad it's gone.

Pointless drivel that just says nothing at least of any import.

The trap was set, words the bait and you were easily caught.

Why oh why can I not fly?

Said the broken ninja butterfly.

You can fly said a strangely normal sort of guy.

Silhouetted by the moon in the midnight sky.

Do you remember him in the hobnail suit?

Watching the bear eating peach tree root.

No worries probably nonsense like most of which I spoke.

Now back to that opinion that it shouldn't be fun I poke.

Or poke that I fun one or the other or the other or one.

I'm not sure anymore of what I previously spun.

The screws holding my head on have just come undone.

So I'll have to leave quickly before it falls off.

In case I start to laugh or even more dangerously cough.

So long farewell and just remember still.

Nothing that just happened was illegal or against your will.

Back into reality slow down you will not get there faster.

Don't Pass Audit Prg Uber Liebe René's Caine Master, Master.

CASH MONEY

So next time you go shopping try to use paper money.

These days shopping's a bit of a joke the kind that isn't funny.

They really want to force us to buys things digitally.

Not so much local shops but those in the oligopoly.

They can govern the things you can
purchase in a cashless society.

The cream on the top of their rancid minds
their usual impropriety.

The black market would simply disappear
if no one accepted cash.

So where would the likes of me buy our
cannabis flowers or hash.

The homeless people on the streets would very soon be dead.

Without begging for cash money, they'd have no daily bread.

Some people think they only exist on heroin, spice and beer.

Probably because they seem to listen but never actually hear.

Those holier than thou that maybe support
charity but to a beggar would never give.

Speaking of things they know nothing about
not caring about how people live.

If you regularly support some charities I
would think by now you know

Although hopefully some of it does do good lots
goes on admin and paying the CEO

Money used to have some value when they had a gold reserve.

Now it's just some numbers an illusion a mystery they preserve.

So, when you go out shopping to buy the things you need.

Go to the places that accept your cash don't
let these fuckers succeed.

They told us viruses got passed on with money made of paper.

Then presented you with a paper receipt
that logic is as solid as vapour.

Career politicians I wouldn't trust not
even as far as I could throw.

It's just a career they're not in it for you
a fact you ought to know.

When one comes along with different ideas
the sort that you could trust.

They grab hold of his or her reputation and throw it under a bus.

Theyfeel very secure in their power as they held it for so long.

We remember the word revolution but just as a line of a song.

So, what can we do? You would need to ask
a cleverer person than me.

When they hold the keys to the kingdom
there is little autonomy.

The keys to the kingdom is a metaphor for
there isn't a kingdom lock.

They hold us back like the shepherds they
are controlling the sleeping flock.

SCALES

When I sit and listen to, watch or read the news.

I wonder if the world's population default is set on snooze.

I mean of course there is always something going on.

All about a ginger prince which while funny is still wrong.

Insomuch as it's everywhere so what are they hiding?

Will it just be some words in legalese or fully law abiding.

In law no victim no crime but legal just isn't the same.

Illegal is breaking a contract where profit and control is the aim.

Legal deals in fiction lawful deals in facts.

Lawful is by tradition but legal by parliament acts.

Often set by corrupt politicians with lobbyists at their heels.

Bribing them almost openly while
continuing to grease the wheels.

Sing a song a sixpence a pocket full of nails

If legal isn't lawful which one tips the scales.

THE GREAT

toilet roll depression

The first great toilet roll depression of the 21st century.

The shelves were all empty although there was plenty.

It originated in Australia where the stocks were short.

But an overblown social media worldwide news report.

Blew the whole damn thing out of proportion.

A very cleverly orchestrated media distortion.

In Australia most of the loo roll is made in China.

So, the world shortage was invented by a social panic designer.

Making the new weird order all about me, me, me.

Divide and conquer as always honestly can't you see?

It seemed that someone believed they
had to curtail our freedom.

The government's had started to realise
we really didn't need them.

They were witnessing worldwide an air of dissent.

Putting fear into those behind the government.

A new weird order was dawning the people all went mental.

So those in charge came down hard and made us all fragmental.

THE GARDEN OF ENGLAND

Kent

The garden of England as once it was called.

But they cut down the hedges and ploughed the land bald.

Outside of Folkestone down near the coast.

A wondrous place the locals would boast.

The natural landscape a sight to be scene.

Breath-taking, stunning, nature serene.

But they wanted a tunnel to go under the sea.

The perfect place for the tunnel to be.

Was all the planners could actually see.

But don't worry folks with the greatest of care.

We'll move the flora to a place over there.

It's a fool proof system tested and tried.

Well actually not so essentially, he lied.

When they moved it the flora withered and died.

The newly homeless wildlife looked at the concrete and cried.

Then a few years later it suddenly got much worse.

A present for brexshit international lorry park curse.

Concrete stretching as far as the eye can see.

Customs checking Lorries now that our country is free.

From that old demon Europe, you know
the good ole brexshit thing.

Is it borders? Is it health? The security of all
or merely kerching, kerching.

Money rolls up to the top of the pile.

Ignoring gravity at least for a while.

Humpty Dumpty sat on a wall eating her ripe banana.

'Brexshit' she said to the man with no head
'You're a right fucking charmer'.

Then came the dark times from deep in the night.

Accompanying the usual terrors and Fright.

There was talk of invasion though it wasn't at the coast.

But we got brexshit done they continue to somehow boast.

We must secure all our borders and make our own laws.

Said the man with no plan to tumultuous applause.

Migrant centres all bursting at the seams.

Visited by a ministers in its fat limousines.

But quick look behind you it's Okay I don't bite.

Oh, and as per usual I really just wrote all that shite.

That sometimes goes nowhere except when it does.

That only rhymes with fuzz, buzz and scuzz.

So, I'll finish this off as it's now gobbledygook
and it looks likes it ain't getting better.

And to sum it all up in a nutshell U...is only a letter.

VEGAN POEM

When I say that I'm vegan and hear disgruntled voices

Is it that people are scared of my personal lifestyle choices

I only say I'm vegan because that's just what I am

And I guess they don't really believe the ingredients of spam

Or perhaps they love a bag of those sticky jelly sweets

Without believing they're made of lips and bums and feet

If you say that you love all animals but couldn't give up meat

An ethical dilemma could be something for you to beat

I wouldn't ever dream of suggesting that you be like me

But tell me that I should eat meat again, get back in the sea

It's not my place to say that you shouldn't be eating corpses

It's just, as you seem to like it so much, why
not cats and dogs and horses?

If you think that that's offensive, I really could care less

If I'm prodding at a guilty conscience and appearing like a pest

Don't bother telling me animals die in order to produce my food

That's a blatant Carnist argument and it's very, fucking rude

They die because the farmers only want to make a buck

As for killing wildlife off in the process they do not give a fuck

The nutritional content of vegan food is a
thing most folks will not know

But unlike the food in a Carnists diet it's very easy to grow

It takes 26% of terrestrial land or at least the land not frozen

To cater for the diet the majority of people have chosen

But being a vegan is more than the food
and definitely more than a diet

And probably why vegans want everyone one to
know and I'm glad that they aren't quiet

It's much more of an ethical viewpoint on the sanctity of life

Whether murdered in a sterile slaughterhouse
or a shed with a rusty old knife

Murder is murder and could never be humane

Although if you really think it is perhaps you are insane

Then the amount of land used to farm the
food for the 'edible' creatures to eat

It's 80% of the planet's farmland and quite a figure to beat

If I had half an acre of land I could grow everything that I need

And I wouldn't kill off any creature because
I'm happy to share my seed

POLITICAL STEW

Another bowl of right-wing political stew.

So what does that mean for the likes of me and you?

More robbing the poor to give to the rich.

Maybe Dennis Moore wasn't a silly bitch.

Like they claimed in a Monty Python episode

Dennis wanted lupines this lot might explode.

Leader out, leader in, leader out, leader in.

Leader out again, take that one on your chin.

Will this one be for better or for worse?

Tightening up of the public purse.

Cutting services and slimming down of spending.

Austerity two is here patent no longer pending.

Reducing the payments to the already loaded.

Who'll pick up the pieces after it's exploded.

Once again, they'll have to borrow more loot.

From the unknown banker in its invisibility suit.

NO NEWS

is good news

I don't read the papers and don't watch the news.

So, my thoughts and opinions aren't anyone's views.

Except of course they are obviously my own.

I mean I know there's a new fossil on the throne.

And Copout 27 they all went to by plane.

Not travelling en masse but then they're all insane.

They won't really be trying to bring about change.

Over six hundred of them at least and this is quite strange.

Were fossil fuel lobbyists they obviously won't.

Although the world's governments also obviously don't.

There are famines and tsunami and hurricanes galore.

They need to act now to even the score.

The balance has shifted it will soon be too late.

To repair all that damage should be not up for debate.

But what's to be done and not targets for the future.

It needs doing now and with more than a suture.

They allow this to continue, and it must be for gain.

That they think we're all stupid is so very plain.

So, I'm not unaware of the things going on.

I just don't listen to the hypnotic media song.

Made up last night in a meeting of minds.

To keep us controlled so we toe the line.

If we do decide to cross it there's hell to pay.

We could if we united make this go away.

But divided we are and divided we stay.

To toe that oppressive line yet another day.

Humble is a good way for a person to be.

Humbled though it's not just mere slavery.

Everyone downtrodden so no one says no.

This system of government just has to go.

Leaving the power in the hands of these fools.

They make it all up then break their own rules.

They have no idea how the rest of us live.

They've done nothing wrong so what's to forgive?

That's how they see it at least I think they do.

But I'm making it up so it's only my view.

Just as you all do in the news that you read.

Or watch whatever and don't see the seed.

They have hidden for you there in plain sight.

And just because I made it up,

doesn't mean it isn't right.

A TYPICAL SUNDAY MORNING

It was Sunday morning my brain was swirly.

I drunk my drink bright and early.

While grinding up powder for future use.

I realise I'm being a tad obtuse.

I've looked at my notes and it's my diagnosis.

I'm away with the fairies perhaps by osmosis.

What's he building in there? I hear them complain.

So, I turn up the volume again and again.

If you know me you'll know I'm not a chocolate fan.

It feels like it burns my mouth and swells my glands.

But occasionally though with some extra bits.

The sort of stuff that gets me off my tits.

I could've spilt some in my coffee I suppose.

Or perhaps it was the butter, goodness only knows.

Whatever it was I'm still totally sane.

All of me well apart from my brain.

But that's an entirely different thing.

Be it benderskum blah, blah, blah or String.

Or whoever happens to be in there this week.

If you unzip my face, you could well get a peak.

But trust, don't do it, that view is quite bleak.

So, it isn't really something of which we speak.

There is one thing though that's proper amazing.

And if I had such stuff probably even hair raising.

I'm actually almost kind of not in my standard massive pain.

Well I am but my brain thinks I like it. I told you it was insane.

Or maybe it's merely a stroke of luck.

Unlike the rest of us we're sane as fuck.

We're the sanest people in this flat.

And all seven of us agree with that.

That includes Walter Travolta you've probably not heard of him.

Not been around since my boxing days
spends all his time in the gym.

String You obviously know already and
maybe you've heard of Glyn.

He's the one with the hunchback and rather fond of gin.

He lives in his laboratory in the cellar under my house.

Apart from the odd explosion he's quiet as a mouse.

To be honest he's not all that friendly
and never welcomes guests.

They interrupt his thought patterns, so
he looks upon them as pests.

My advice except in a medical emergency
is don't go there just avoid him.

However, he'll fix you up proper even if you need a new limb.

The others I've probably not mentioned
before for that there is a reason.

There's a time and place for everything
but this is not their season.

Sing a song a sixpence a pocket full of sewage and shit.

Dumped there by water companies I don't
doubt that one little bit.

Four and twenty that reminds me of
something to which I've been.

I know that it was in London, but it wasn't to look for a queen.

It was in a park I remember bought a T-shirt from a Rasta bloke.

Sat and had a blah, blah, blah shared each other's smoke.

When a young guy came and asked us
where he could buy some weed.

I implied that I may well be fed he looked
at me straight then fled.

The dude said that was evil bro, you are dreader than dredd.

That was a wicked day but something bad happened of course.

One of our popo protectors got thrown
to the ground by it's horse.

The horse was unharmed in the end I'm
sure you'll be glad to hear.

Using poor horses with a popo astride to instil a sense of fear.

It grinds all my gears because it just isn't right.

To subject those poor horses to such an awful plight.

Sing a song a sixpence my pockets loaded with cash.

I've done all those things for you gods, queens
and kings and now I's gotta dash.

Toedeledoki

A VIRUS

with shoes

There is a deadly virus that's spread throughout the land.

Its catalyst human nature I hope you'll understand.

It is nature versus nurture slash and burn insanity.

A virus with shoes destroying the planet its name is humanity.

The world is getting warmer of that there can be no doubt.

Unless we ignore all the news about heat
waves, wildfires and droughts.

If you know why we live in a temperate land.

This is something you'll likely understand.

We get our warmish climate due to the North Atlantic Drift.

When the polar ices have melted this will most likely shift.

The colder seas sink to the bottom which
drags the warmer ones up.

When this exchange stops happening us lot are out of luck.

Our winters will be awful, storms and bitter cold.

Not somewhere nice to live if you're sick or frail or old.

Time to end all the discussions take proper measures now.

Not another copout whatever that seems clueless as to how.

Flying from every corner of the Earth no doubt by private jet.

Destroying the planet bit by bit so they haven't started yet.

There are several climate tipping points
that now appear as certainty.

Yet the politicians that make decisions don't
get the concept of urgently.

If all the promises given by world leaders at copout 26.

Were followed to the letter the targets would still get missed.

The minimum temperature rise will still
be one and a half degrees.

Whatever they promised isn't enough to
stop the rising of the seas.

The permafrost with its planet warming gases is thawing.

For fucks sake humanity consider that a warning.

It holds they estimate over fifty years'
worth of our current emissions.

Did you hear there's a climate crisis or
didn't you bother to listen.

There's an ice sheet in the Antarctic that's ready to break away.

If it does the seas will rise twenty-five inches in less than a day.

This would be likely to cause freak climate
events almost anywhere.

Will you wait till your house is underwater
before you actually care?

If you've settled and live near the sea the
prospect for you is grim.

And if you live in the lowlands you'd better learn to swim.

There's a huge carbon sink called the Amazon
Forest constantly under attack.

Its resources have always been finite, and it isn't growing back.

At some time in the distant future, they'll
look back at now and say.

Those foolish homoconsumerus were blind to a better way.

Then there is of course the sea, humanities seafood larder.

We'll rid the oceans of all its life if we try a little bit harder.

We'll fill it with our sewage and our endless plastic waste.

Which of us will be the winner of this destructive human race?

The waterways continuously filling from
pipes attached to the sewers.

They'll make a documentary about it for
the late, late, late show viewers.

I caught a glimpse of some blah, blah, blah earlier on the news.

Easy to mute and ignore give my brain a snooze.

I'm powerless, there's nothing I can do
you'll be conditioned to believe.

Cast that off, know you can,

a tree only starts as a seed.

TOWERS

i

We

cAn't

BUiLD

TOWERs

FOReVER

fOUNdATIOnS

HoWeER CHaOtiC
ArE VItAL FoR groWTH

UNLIKE PLANTS OUR ROOTS

HAVE SOCIAL MOBILITY SO CHOICE

Here or there or there or there or there or anywhere

YOUR ROOTS BELONG WHERE YOU HAVE A VOICE

SNOW NONSENSE

So did it actually snow? No, there's no such fucking thing.

Unlike of course my invisible friends especially good old String.

We've been with Scribbler for ever and here's something you won't know.

We homogenised quietly in a jungle a year or sixty ago.

No one else can fully see us and it's always been that way.

He thought we were the only ones; till the others came to stay.

However, I'm sure that's nothing special and you lot have invisible friends.

If not, I think I best warn you round here that's round the bend.

Oh, you're not from round here are you? I often here folks say.

No and the way you lot are to everything I wouldn't want to stay.

When I say everything, I mean exactly that.

Give you a priceless antique you'll turn it into tat.

You don't need a wicket keeper as they've privatised the bat.

Cricket however has forty two rules; make what you want of that.

TOMATO TOMAYTO

We need well-being, happiness, high-virtue, and right moral action.

Plato's philosophy for a fair society to achieve true satisfaction.

Well-being is a thing that could easily be achieved.

If we didn't have leaders that can never be believed.

Unfortunately, that's how it and maybe what we deserve.

Conservatives aren't conservation for there's nothing they conserve.

Except of course the bank balances of them and all their mates.

I guarantee there'll be no shortages on parliamentary plates.

We have a fake tomato shortage nothing on the shelves.

The bloody Europeans have kept them for themselves.

Well maybe not but the weather there is really bad.

So, they thankfully sent a few boxes to keep cabinet ministers glad.

Another idiot minister said eat turnips instead they're great.

Pizza made with turnip sauce trust I just can't wait.

Last year it was a petrol shortage or at least a shortage of drivers

Then they gave emergency visas to people that are not like us skivers.

What we really don't need is a government entirely of pound shop Macgyvers.

When the rats desert this sinking ship there'll probably be no survivors.

Energy prices went exponentially high.

While brexshit benefits were pie in the sky.

But back to the tomatoes missing from the shelves.

It's not Europeans keeping them for themselves.

Lorries coming to blighty wait seventy-seven hours to clear.

So, none of the produce is even fresh by the time it reaches here.

Although this is all in my head and therefore matters not.

It's nothing to do with me that the world has gone to pot.

Kent is being covered in tarmacadam

Those brexshit benefits we.ve already had em.

Hark, hark the dogs do bark.

We needed a customs lorry park.

So, they cut down the orchards here in Kent.

To deliver the plans of the government.

When I say plans, I mean vaguely formed thoughts.

Meanwhile lorries are clogging up the ports.

Traffic jams on every inbound road.

Welcome to blighty our humble abode.

LAW

& DiSOrdEr

If you grow your own cannabis, it's still at schedule one.

But if you know the truth you know that, that is dumb.

Medicinal properties it has none is the
definition of schedule one.

But cannabis grown under licence inside not under the sun.

Miraculously has medicinal properties so
it seems a tale has been spun.

There is no difference in species just like in other plants.

All plants have sub species or varieties it's
part of nature's fabulous dance.

So logically if there is no difference between
legal or homegrown weed.

The reason for the law is political ideology
holding hands with corporate greed.

I talk to people all the time about my personal use of pot.

That often didn't know it was legal so still believed it's not.

Not just the people I speak to police officers often don't know.

The real government that actually run the
country like that status quo.

Most people I talk with agree that the change
in the law should be made obvious.

And the fact that it could be illegal to grow any
kind of plant is nothing short of ridiculous.

They made it legal for legal medical clinics to sell.

In the process corporation bank balances swell.

To them it's a bit of a joke they don't even need the money'

But, for those who are ill or unable to work
that joke just isn't funny.

The money and resources that they have and continue to lose.

On this failed drug war that the government continue to choose.

It could have been put to a much better use
and that is without a question.

That it gets nibbled away at right down the line
I wouldn't make that suggestion.

First of all, free the weed and anyone in prison for an unjust law.

Ideological political prisoners' casualties in a failed drug war.

But give us our back our plant for a start.

End prohibition its rotten at the heart.

Stop wasting police time.

No victim no crime.

The Misuse of Drugs Act or MoDA , what a weird little acronym

For a substance to be considered as controlled
it would have to be very grim.

A dangerous drug to be avoided and very harmful to health.

Except for scientific research shouldn't even be on the shelf.

For cannabis to be labelled dangerous as such.

Is just fantasy land and they know as much.

However back in the sixties with 1964 in fact.

A MP made a ten-minute bill that soon became an act.

That cited synthesised cannabinol a dangerous drug indeed.

Synthesised cannabinoids are dangerous
but they don't come from a seed.

Cannabis grows from a seed but those were produced in a lab.

Trying to get to the truth of it is like continually picking a scab.

The way the bill was worded was to very cleverly deflect.

Which is why to me the law is false and
deserves no kind of respect.

To them it's all just politics and to them
all part of the political game.

They need to be made accountable and

then do the walk of shame.

Cannabis caregiver growers can still go to prison for years.

So, the law is a postcode lottery at least that's how it appears.

Just like in any community there is always some division.

It helps them maintain this status quo a very political decision.

They are losing this war against a plant
so they ought to call a truce.

Cannabis is a product of nature and should
be legal whatever the use.

Personally, I am a Cantheist and consider it my human right.

To use this plant for the good of my world
and for that I am willing to fight.

Politicians if you don't give us back that
which our whole world needs.

Legal rights to produce our own medication
and to grow our wonderful seeds.

When it's next time to vote, just remember this.

You'll be at the bottom if you're even on the list.

SMALL BOATS

or no hope

People must be desperate coming here in small boats.

If they arrive in these flimsy vessels that are hardly even afloat.

Then they are arrested and detained till the paperwork is done.

It wasn't this way however before brexshit was begun.

Have they always come here this way
was something I wondered

In seems in 2018 total similar crossings
were a mere three hundred.

It seems there is no legal route for asylum seekers to use.

It's an act of desperation whatever they do they lose.

Live in a war zone or come here I know which I would choose.

Some people call it invasion those with narrow minded views.

People don't sign contracts when they
fear for their lives and flee.

So there is no rule on remaining in the first safe country.

That's just some propaganda to make you despise them more.

While pretending that for real refugees there is an open door.

They deliberately label them migrants to denigrate their case.

By they I mean the government that lie right to your face.

Small boat crossings are rising 30,000 last year.

Probably about to rise even more with the
latest announcement fear.

The gangs that operate the crossings will
tell the refugees to hurry.

They tell them new laws are coming soon
so they really need to worry.

Buy your passage very quick or soon you'll be too late to stay.

Effectively speeding up the timeframe in which the victims pay.

STILL NO SNOW

It seems once more the fake snow photos
are coming out of the closet

And whether or not you believe in it you will
have definitely lost your deposit

On sensibility that is because the thing you ought to know

Is it's a thing of the past so nowadays
there's no such thing as snow

Unless of course you live somewhere
that it actually isn't banned

Here in blighty by the government the weather is fully planned

Ok that the government actually plans
is obviously not really true

They throw some ideas into a hat and pull out what they'll do

Don't bother sending pictures of what you think is snow

The country is fully hipponotised I think you ought to know

Part of the ready baked brexshit farce snow has been outlawed

If you wish to see actual snow you'll have to travel abroad

I have it appears an imagination that some feel a bit far fetched

But if you believe snow still exists here yours is overstretched

I'm looking out the window and all I can honestly say

I believe in sleet and hail and rain and that here its eternally grey

So, sing a song of sixpence a pocket full of sleet and hail

Try to convince me that snow is here I'm
afraid you're going to fail

HISTORY

and...in case you forgot

I'd like to tell you a very short story about a bunch of crooks.

But you'll never see what crimes they did in your history books.

They were businessmen and government
and many more besides.

They're still out there in the open in plain sight they all hide.

I'm talking about the prohibitionists I've
mentioned them all before.

A little over a century ago when people didn't know the score.

It all began with William Hearst.

I said before he was one of the first.

He was a blatantly a racist, but in those
days, it was seen as normal.

He blamed all his problems on Mexicans in
his papers to make it formal.

Rockefeller was another who had the herbalists all shut down.

Then flooded the world with P Harmacies dirty drugs in town.

Andrew Mellon financed them all a banker
and secretary of state.

Another the owner of General Motors who also owned DuPont.

In history books decent citizens they can
make up whatever they want.

ECS

The Endocannabinoid system is a part of every vertebrate.

I'll do my best to explain it to you if you're willing to wait.

It produces endogenous lipid retrograde neurotransmitters.

Looking after our lesser systems a bit like babysitters.

It has more than two types of receptors but CB1 and CB2.

Are the ones that are known of mostly
and to which I have a clue.

Endo means from within our bodies phyto is from plants.

THC activates the system when the law just give it a chance.

The Helpful Cannabinoid is the one.

That starts stuff off and gets things done.

THC is necessary for our bodies to achieve homeostasis.

Without it the system runs but not on a proper solid basis.

Though one of them mimics the other chemically
they're not just different in name.

Unlike THC and CBD components which are
chemically exactly the same.

The reason they have different properties is
because of how they're arranged.

And if this stuff all sounds baffling trust, I agree that it's strange.

THC is the Phytocannabinoid that mimics anandamide.

What Anandamide does from within THC mimics from outside.

Just like its Endo version it binds to CB1 in the brain.

And also, the rest of the nervous system
the places we experience pain.

Whereas 2-AG as it's called for short CB2 receptors constrain.

CB2 are found in the places pain is normally made.

And regulate our bodily function systems a very handy trade.

The mimetic phyto here seemingly says it Can't Be Done.

It blocks the CB2 receptors and now my head is spun.

This one you'll no doubt have heard of its known as CBD.

But without The Helpful Cannabinoid it ain't no good to me.

I'm not trying to say CBD is bad but it's
better with the full entourage.

But those people who vilify THC are guilty of canna sabotage.

So, to summarise this stuff it's safe to say I'd
need to be very much cleverer.

But I'm just a simple benderskum and not a university lecturer.

And although I understand some of this stuff,
I'm really not the cleverest bloke.

But can feel it doing me a power of good
when I eat it or just take a toke.

HAIRBRAIN

There once was a man with hair and a brain

If you met him now, he's bald but quite sane

Not that I'm suggesting he wasn't before

But he was more hirsute and that is for sure

I'm aware many people may think he's mad

He lives in his own world and that makes him glad

Believing his truth that the whole worlds a shop

He only indulges them hoping one day they'll stop

Nothing he makes is meant for sale although
somehow some does get sold

Not by him though he'd have you know
in a tale he's so often told

What he finds most astounding is that
people would want to buy

His books or his scribble as in his opinion
they're only Pi in the sky

Thinks he sounds clever and only gives the
appearance he might be cool

But trust me I know him really well, he's
an idiot but still not a fool

Anyway, none of that blah, blah, blah was

anything to do with this story

He's honest I can tell you that for sure so obviously not a tory

Many years ago, in the days he still had hair

He lived deep in the woods a lush life if you dare

But that's another story too, I know you couldn't make this up

The sort you could spin in front of a fire
with a spliff and a full coffee cup

Now the next bit may well be fantasy
alternatively it may well be true

How far you are willing to expand reality is entirely up to you

One late summer night fast asleep many years ago

Amongst the trees under the stars the fire merely afterglow

An oddly glowing wasp landed on his
head and crawled into his ear

He never even stirred a bit you may well be surprised to hear

The wasp laid her eggs dozens of them
translucent and nearly microscopic

Incidentally I know I digress but whilst we're on the topic

With a balloon and some papier-mâché
make yourself a fake wasp nest

Where you hang it, wasps will avoid instead of being a pest

But back to what I was saying before, the wasp then flew away

Next morning drinking fresh roasted coffee
from the jug bubbling on the fire

Rolled a big fat spliff of Hindu Kush so that
day he was gonna start higher

The wasp eggs completely dormant all

day so nothing seemed amiss

He went about his peaceful day ignorance certainly bliss

Everything was kushty all day long but
that night when he was asleep

The eggs all hatched simultaneously and headed into the deep

Next morning, he woke up dizzier than
usual and couldn't work out why

His vision weird and blurry so thought something must be awry

So off he went to town, which was seven miles to have a bath

He did this about twice a month actually no, I'm having a laugh

When he arrived at the dead-end centre
the staff became concerned

They showed him in a mirror his eyes
look like they'd been burned

They sent him to the hospital but on the journey there

The ambulance was involved in a massive
pile up and that was quite a scare

He decided to visit a witch he knew she lived in another wood

This sort of thing was up her path and she'd fix him if she could

She said she knew the symptoms and
could easily make him well

But that would leave him indebted to her
so basically under her spell

There really wasn't another choice though
he still didn't know what it was

Yes, he agreed but what was occurring he
needed to know because...

She explained that there were maggot
wasps nibbling at his brain

That's why everything is a bit skewwhiff
as if you're going insane

Don't worry though I've a cure for sure but timing is essential

If not, everything becomes too big and
you become their residential

That's not even something she wanted to consider

She had a plan she said the ACME maggot wasp get ridder

First, she had to shave his head but she kept all of his hair

In a jar on a shelf in the corner somewhere over there

She bade him come and sit down here and then to his surprize

He couldn't move a muscle not even blink his eyes

She told him please don't be afraid you've
just been hipponotised

She told him he wouldn't feel a thing she guaranteed no pain

We need to do something to stop the
creatures eating all of ypour brain

She opened up a drawer took out what looked like a drill

She said it was a laser auger and asked if he needed a pill

She made 42 perfectly circular 6 mil holes
in his newly shaven head

She told him there was nothing to worry about
and it's better than being dead

He couldn't move a muscle and didn't feel a thing

She opened a purple container with 42 tiny rats within

She removed the little blighters carefully one by one

Then with perfect precision held them twixt finger and thumb

She put one in each of the holes and before they gave her the slip

She clamped their long tails together in a very special clip

Then it was down to timing and keeping an eye on things

Hoping not to reach the point when the legendary fat lady sings

But things didn't go quite as planned and
the rats ate far too much

Not able to pull them back out of the holes
completely stuck as such

Leaving him with what could only be
called rats tails instead of hair

But he didn't even own a mirror so it's not as though he'd care

The rats of course had to be poisoned the doctors called it chemo

But if you've percevered till this far along,
you'll know that it may not be so

LEGAL WEED

in the UK?

I've been a cannabis activist for many, many years

When the government said it was legal I didn't believe my ears

I'm known as a proper cynic so doubted it was true

I now know I was wrong so let me explain to you

I got in touch with a clinic there are several now to use

Thought I'd try to get a prescription I had nothing really to lose

It's really not that difficult I suggest you give a try

For cannabis is legal now honestly no word of a lie

The Journey is fairly easy to get you legal access

A referral from your doctor is the beginning of the process

Next it is an online meeting with a
specialist cannabis consultant

To decide if cannabis can help with a
prescription as the possible resultant

Then they have a meeting to discuss your medical need

To decide if they think you'll benefit from cannabis oil or weed

My prescription is for oil and buds so my pains are now relieved

If I hadn't ventured down this road I never would have believed

It isn't any dearer than what is on the street

Having legal access is somewhat hard to beat

OLIGOPOLY

Let me be clear right from the start some rules cannot be broken

Yes, you may well think they can but what of the ones unspoken

Exactly! You don't even know what they
are however they still exist

Try as much as you like to disobey them,
but know this you can't resist

For resistance is futile especially on this particular occasion

You don't know what you're resisting so
don't need my persuasion

Let me tell you now to bring you up to speed

That thing you're not resisting is the usual corporate greed

It's illegal for an individual or company
to have a trade monopoly

Did you know though the supermarkets
here are part of an oligopoly

Which means they set the prices and dictate what you can buy

The notion of a buyer's choice is proper Pi in the sky

The only way beat them is don't buy from them shop around

Farm shops and independents can give you more for your pound

Supermarkets would rather destroy imperfect
food than give it to the needy

If you get right down at the root of it, they
are quintessentially greedy

They create a deliberate shortage by not restocking some shops

Wait for one complaint then suddenly the news flash drops

Due to some unavoidable problem there's
a shortage of this and that

With factors completely beyond our
control. Don't you smell a rat?

They'll blame it on the weather or maybe a tidal wave

Something really stinks round here but it
might just be my after-shave

One problem in this country the oligopoly
dictates the price they'll pay

So, farmers selling locally for more would prefer to sell that way

Selling to us only when the price at their market is less

How did it ever get this bad every things a total mess

Besides when customs can take over seventy hours to clear

I imagine less of them want to ship their fresh goods over here

And can they really be considered fresh
so long after being cropped?

Decay begins at the moment they are or
hasn't that penny dropped?

It's weird that you vote in a government to
decide things on your behalf

Yet lobbyists hold their attention far longer
is funny but not for a laugh

The ones that throw the most lavish parties
and probably some other bonus

Not an honest soul amongst them Diogenes'
lamp would have shown us

BENDERDRIVEL THE SERIES SO FAR

A larger pile of utter drivel has yet to be seen

What's In A Benderskum: Some Stuff I Think About Dotted With Scribbles Minus Colour

The thoughts poems and scribbles of a benderskum

String's Book Of Benderskum: From A Different Perspective

A book of writings, poems and scribbles by a benderskum

The Six Legged Spider Of Memory And Some Other Drivel

More nonsense better out than in

Benderskribbles: And A Touch Of Rhyming Drivel

A larger size than a paperback more graphic novel size full of scribbles in colour and some other drivel

I'm Merely A Benderskum So What Would I Know...: However

A virtually complete collection of my poems to date

August 2021

Benderskum ' S..T..Inks: Methinks

the usual mix of scribble and words inks this time

Yet More Drivel

poetry and drivel and an updated version of The Six Legged
Spider of Memory

THE LAST WORD

I was intending to show pictures
of all the covers, unfortunately but
there was a thingummy glitch
Never mind, even though they're better than
the content I deleted them without a hitch

ABOUT THE AUTHOR

Rocky Van De Benderskum & Co

So first of all we are the author we mean just because these are our thoughts at best or at worst thoughts we've had albeit ours or otherwise so we might or might not be the author. Certainly the two fingered typist that's for sure

We would put a picture but that bit glitched so not

butone of us is on the cover sitting on a three legged stool the night we escaped

The stuff in this book has or will be shown on the radio in a radio show called benderdrivel on

www.radio-illumini.com

Printed in Great Britain
by Amazon